- **Letters to Will Series** -

Letter 5:
JESUS Was a Feminist and Much Much More

A Grandfather's Guide to Life

Leonard Swidler, PhD (Grandfather)

Letters to Will Series

Letter 5: Jesus Was a Feminist...and Much More

By Leonard Swidler, PhD

This book is available as an individual volume. Visit https://ipubcloud.com/product/jesus-was-a-feminist-and-much-much-more/

You are invited to join in the conversation.

As I sit down to welcome you into this continued conversation between my granddaughter, Will, and myself, I would like to bring you up to date. This is the second book of a series, Letters to Will.

You may know by now, I'm a Professor of Interreligious Dialogue at Temple University, but I am also a grandpa and I take my position in this young woman's life very seriously. Writing about life's lessons in the first book was an area of thought that I had pondered for years, but when her questions turned to religion, that which I am also well-versed in, I wanted to give her a view of richness that not all have experienced.

So, through stories and questions, we bring you this book. I chose these stories to give you a different depth of understanding of this man named Jesus and how it relates to our lives today.

Religion is a subject that we could write and discuss for years, and many would never, ever reach its deepest core. But in these pages, we can experience the true humanity of Jesus.

Will and I are thrilled that you have joined us on this journey. We welcome you.

About iPubCloud.com

You've opened the right book from the iPub international library. You might be a scholar, an avid reader, a mother or father, a teacher, a 'tween or teen, or one of the rest of us.

Welcome home to iPub Global Connection where knights of old and now digital nomads from all over the world meet safely to share ideas, find resources, and support individuals whose voices wish to be heard to create and protect the world for your great, great grandchildren.

We are committed to the empowerment of each and all individuals' contributions to a better world. Often, we feel paralyzed by our limiting doubt that alone we have no ability or opportunity to make any real impact. When that thought comes up, pick up your eraser in your mind's eye and say "backspace, delete." Individually, together, we can and will influence causing the important changes to ensure a habitable world for 3 generations….a world embracing global citizenship one by one.

How would *you* begin to define global citizenship? One way might be to be open enough to learn about other cultures and peoples so that we can connect with all. There are, of course, many ways—through music, art, blogs, podcasts, philosophy, all of which help children model how to be better citizens.

Here you may find what you're looking for, the idea you'd like to expand...a place to be open, to learn, and to trust.

Read on and become a part of the ongoing conversations. Email a note, comment or share your idea or blog post. Don't keep your views or us a secret. Your voice counts and we care.

This world is in dire need of love, patience and respect and iPub Publishing is a place where you may find a sentinel in the direction to achieve this transformation. We, along with you, can be a guide towards world peace, improving communication through dialogue, advancing diplomacy among nations to engage with differences. Our international writers, authors, thinkers, and scholars are here to make you think....**Join the renaissance!**

iPub Global Connection, LLC
www.iPubCloud.com
550 W. Baseline Rd., #303
Mesa, AZ 85210
info@iPubCloud.com

Copyright © 2019 Leonard Swidler
Cover Design by Arewa Abiodun Ibrahim
Cover Photo by Leonard Swidler Other iPub Global Connection books may be found at https://www.ipubcloud.com

Table of Contents

Introduction 1

Letter No. 5: Jesus Was a Feminist…
and Much More! 2

1. What Feminism Is, and Is Not 8

2. The Pharisee and the Prostitute 12

3. The Rabbi and the Adulteress 18

4. The Missing Story! 24

5. Jesus Really Was a Feminist—So…? 27

6. Looking Forward 28

Introduction

"Will" is short for Willow Athena Swidler-Notte, my fantastic grand-daughter, born at the beginning of the Third Millennium (2000). I have been going to her home practically every weekend since 2011, to teach her German (which is why I am addressed as *Opa*, a typical German abbreviation for Grandpa). We talk about all kinds of interesting things in life—and end up having dinner with Will and my brilliant daughter Eva and her wonderful husband Ian. Both are professors, Ian, a high school ecology and biology teacher, and Eva, a university history teacher.

These are my letters to Will, with whom—when you meet her, you will understand why—I clearly am madly in love.

Len Swidler, (info@ipubcloud.com)

Letter No. 5: Jesus Was a Feminist... and Much More!

Dear Will,

There are two explanations that you should know about before we begin. For one, you will see little numbers that look like they are connected to a word. These are called footnotes. If you click on the number, a window will open and give you additional information where you can find even more information about what you just read. (Or, look to the bottom of the printed page.) Fun, isn't it?

Another important explanation is how we refer to Bible verses and to show them in books that I write. A little bit of background before I describe the method. The word Bible was derived from the ancient Phoenician (present day Lebanon) coastal city, Byblos, where the papyrus reeds from along the Nile river in Egypt were shipped to be pressed and transformed into "paper" (papyrus), sheets of which, when sewn together formed a "book" (from Byblos).

The Bible for Jews consists of the Torah [Hebrew word for "teaching"].

The Bible for Christians consists of the "Old Testament"—today, out of respect for the Jewish tradition and the "New Testament" consisting of the four Gospels:

- Matthew
- Mark
- Luke
- John

The four Gospels:

- Writings about the Jew Yeshua [Hebrew for Jesus]
- Paul of Tarsus' letters
- Other early missionaries' writings referring to Jesus as the "Messiah" [In Hebrew: Meshiach and in Greek: Christos meaning the Anointed One.]

References to both the Hebrew Bible and the New Testament are usually presented by an abbreviated form of the subsection, called a "book," followed by the chapter number, and then the verses.

For example, the first book of the Bible, Genesis, would be cited this way:

"Gen 3: 5-9"

The biblical book, Genesis, chapter 3, verses 5 to 9.

I hope this explanation helps you reading this book and the Bible easier. And, as we always say, Will, *Wir werden sehen*! [German for we will see!]

It's interesting, Will, that you ran across a quotation from my long-ago article "Jesus Was a Feminist," which I published nearly a half-century ago![1] Hmm, reminds me, Will, just how old I am getting!

That article was reproduced scores of times and translated into numerous languages. I even published a *New York Times* Op Ed[2] version of it, and many years later followed it up with a large scholarly investigation of the idea that "Jesus really was a feminist."[3] (Actually, Will, I have subsequently been referring to Jesus by his original Hebrew name, *Yeshua*, to help Christians—and others—remember that he was not a Christian, but a Jew and a Rabbi to boot! I will continue to do so in this letter.)

Although I have published more than ninety books, I am certain that I am known by far more persons for that article than all my books put together! Just some recent stories, Will: About five years ago, I was at a meeting at the World Council of Churches in Geneva, Switzerland, and we broke for lunch and went to the cafeteria. I got in line behind a man in his fifties and, while waiting, put my hand out and said, "Hi, I'm Leonard Swidler." He turned and stared at me and in a loud and powerful voice said, *"The* Leonard Swidler!?" Will, I have to say that I was in shock! I mumbled something, and he then pointed a defining finger at me and declared: *"Jesus Was a Feminist!"* Aghast, I stammered, "Where did that come from?" He told me

---

[1] Leonard Swidler, "Jesus Was a Feminist," *Catholic World*, January, 1971, pp. 171-183.
[2] Leonard Swidler, "Jesus Was a Feminist," *New York Times*, December 18, 1971.
[3] Leonard Swidler, *Jesus Was a Feminist. What the Gospels Reveal about His Revolutionary Perspective* (Lanham, MD: Sheed & Ward, 2007).

then that, decades before, his theological seminary professor in Chicago gave out my "Jesus Was a Feminist" essay to read. I reckoned that it must have really seared itself into his memory to have so suddenly and spontaneously produced such an eruption so far away and so long afterward.

Amazingly, Will, this sort of thing still happens to me! A couple years after that event, I was at the annual meeting of the North American Academy of Ecumenists, held that year in the headquarters of the Lutheran Church in Chicago. After a panel presentation, I found myself waiting with one of the panelists for water to heat up for a cup of tea. She was probably in her late thirties, and a professor of theology in a Lutheran Theological Seminary. Well, Will, as I often do, I stuck my hand out and said that I was Leonard Swidler. She looked at me quizzically, and then asked—here it comes again: "The *Jesus Was a Feminist* Leonard Swidler?!" She went on to tell me that, because of the article, she decided to go to seminary, and eventually became a seminary professor. Amazing!

There's more, Will. The reach of that one article has not been restricted to professional theologians. Just three years ago, out of the blue, I received a letter from a successful Catholic business woman. When she was in college in the 1980s, she read my "Jesus Was a Feminist" article and was so inspired by it that she pasted it inside the cover of her Bible, which she read every day. She then wrote that, as the article was getting worn, she decided to replace it—upon which the thought occurred to her that, with the internet and all, she could perhaps find my address and write and thank me. She did just that, saying how much that image of Jesus strengthened her in deciding to start her business career.

As I already said, Will, if I never published another word (just this year, 2019, my scholarly tome *Jesus Was a Feminist* came out in Korean!) I can go to my grave feeling that I made the world a little better for my having been here—and writing: "Jesus Was a Feminist"!

1. What Feminism Is, and Is Not

Will, I know that you have read and heard the term "feminist" many, many times—and not just from me and your mom. Still, maybe it would be good if I would tell you again in plain language what I meant by that term—and what I did not mean!

Let's start with the latter. "Feminist," as the term has been largely used for more than a hundred years, does *not* mean being anti-men. Also, it does not mean women being the *same* as men. **Rather, it means thinking of and treating women as the *equals* of men**—and resisting any and all contrary customs.

Will, as you know quite well, some men can be better than some (or all) women at certain things; conversely, some women can be better than some (or all) men at certain things. So, the obvious smart thing to do is to let everyone—female, male, or in between—do what they do best. Unfortunately, Will, contemporary societies still have a long way to go to make commonplace such an obvious way of thinking and acting.

One male did, in fact, think and act that way long before such an attitude became the conscious goal of a movement. Who? **Rabbi Yeshua ha Notzri—Rabbi Jesus of Nazareth.**

What Feminism Is and Is Not

Will, you might be thinking about now, "Come on, Opa, I have been singing in church choirs for years, so I am more than familiar with negative sayings like, 'Women should keep silent in church,' 'I suffer no woman to have authority over a man,' and 'Wives obey your husbands!' and, and...."

Ah, Will, I am glad to see that you have been paying attention all this time! Those sayings are, embarrassingly, from the New Testament. However, what is important to notice is they were *not* said by Rabbi Yeshua!

Since you know German pretty well, you may also be familiar with a popular old-fashioned German saying which pushes the same basic points in the *non*-Yeshua New Testament: *Kinder, Küche, Kirche*! (Children, Kitchen, Church!). However, that saying doesn't work so well in Germany any more since Dr. Angela Merkel (a Lutheran Pastor's daughter!) has not been spending most of her time caring for her *Kinder*, or in the *Küche*, or the *Kirche* for that matter—since for the past ten years she has been *Frau Doktor Kanzler* (Madam Doctor Chancellor) of Germany, and the most powerful woman in the world!

Well, Will, you are probably thinking: OK, so what did Yeshua do as far as women were concerned that was so egalitarian? I am glad that you are not satisfied with generalities, but want details, facts. So, let me start with a quite dramatic example of when his enemies set out to quash his growing reputation as a *feminist*;

remember, Will, whenever any woman or man tries to do something good, they are also going to proportionately gain enemies!

2. The Pharisee and the Prostitute

As I noted, Will, there are numerous occasions recorded in the Gospels where women are treated by various men as second-class citizens—or less! There are also situations where women were treated by others not at all as persons, but just as sex objects. It was expected that Yeshua would do the same! Those expectations, as we shall see, were deeply disappointed.

One such occasion occurred when Yeshua was invited to dinner at the house of a skeptical Pharisee [Luke 7, 36] and a woman of "ill repute" entered and washed Yeshua's feet with her tears, wiped his feet with her hair, and then anointed them.

Will, you're probably thinking: *Wow*, that's quite a scene—washing this stranger rabbi's feet (with your own tears yet!), drying them with your own hair (double *Wow*!), and them *kissing* them! *Wow* again!

You are right. And it gets even better, for the Gospel writer reports that the Pharisee looked upon her as just a filthy, sexual creature. He (or she) reports: "The Pharisee...said to himself, 'If this man were a prophet, he would know who this woman is who is *touching* him [Will, *that* isn't supposed to happen in that culture!] and what a bad name she has.'" There is no question that the woman—who remains forever

The Pharisee and the Prostitute

nameless—was a prostitute. The text states boldly that she was a "sinner" [*hamartolos: Greek word for sinner*]. But that's not how Rabbi Yeshua reacted. He clearly and deliberately rejected that approach to the woman as a "sex object."

Instead, Yeshua called the Pharisee out! He reminded him that when he came into his house the Pharisee did *NOT* give him the traditional kiss, or arrange to have the dust washed off his feet, or his head anointed, all of which were the custom. Bluntly, Yeshua pointed out (as we saw) that the woman washed his feet—not with regular water, but with her tears!—and dried them not with a towel, but with her hair. Further, she not only provided the missing formal kiss, but gave Yeshua numberless kisses on his feet, and didn't presume to anoint his head—as should have been done by the host—but anointed his feet!

In other words, Will, her actions were precisely what the Pharisee did not do. Yeshua then said to the Pharisee: 'You did not perform those customary courtesies—but she did.' He compared the Pharisee's high and mighty attitude toward the prostitute with her truly "elegant" behavior. She came off as a sensitive hostess and he an offensive man!

The Gospel reports that Rabbi Yeshua spoke directly to the woman. You should know, Will, it was not proper for men to speak in public to women—doubly so for rabbis. But Rabbi Yeshua spoke to the woman as a human person: "Your sins are forgiven.... Your faith has saved you; go in peace."

Hmm, what do you think? Why in the world did that prostitute burst into the house of that Pharisee and throw herself at this Rabbi's feet? Well, remember, Yeshua was doing a lot of street preaching. Because there were no movies, TV, radio, Facebook....nothing else to relieve the drudgery of everyday life, people apparently flocked to spell-binding orators. The Gospels elsewhere mentions there were about 4,000 people listening to Yeshua. I suspect that our "lady of the street" must have heard Rabbi Yeshua speaking, perhaps more than once. She was so moved by him and what he said that she decided to change her life. She then bought some ointment (or perhaps already had some as part of her "regular business") and followed Yeshua into the Pharisee's house. According to the Gospel, the Pharisee knew her reputation. One could wonder whether he might have known her more closely in another context?

Rabbi Yeshua obviously discerned what was going on with the woman—where she "was coming from," as you might put it. That's why he spoke to her about forgiving her sins (*hamartiai: Greek word for sins*). She obviously was in remorseful *agony*—"for she loved much," which is a very insightful, sensitive, compassionate way to speak of a prostitute...Was it a *woman* who noticed and recorded this sensitivity on the part of Yeshua? What do you think, Will? In any

The Pharisee and the Prostitute

case, Yeshua obviously saw her as an independent, decision-making, loving human being!

That Gospel story ends by saying that "they then went in to eat dinner." After what Rabbi Yeshua said, one wonders how the Pharisee enjoyed his meal. For that matter, Will, you may also wonder who was present and who shared all these details about what had just gone on in that house. Among all the dinners this famous preacher must have been invited to and all those people who attended them, who would have thought this occasion important enough to record as a little vignette [Middle French word for story or illustration]? What do you think, Will?

My guess is that it most probably was a woman or group of women (the nameless prostitute herself?) who somehow soaked up the facts and words, and then made sure they were written down. Thus, they eventually ended up in what we today call Luke's Gospel. Maybe one or more of the servant women— Humpf! Who do you think did all the cooking, serving, and cleaning up, Will? Certainly not the men!

I have written a separate book about all that: it asks, where did we get most of the information about Rabbi Yeshua from?[4] Maybe now your curiosity is

---

[4] See Leonard Swidler, *Three Certitudes About Jesus* (Eugene. OR: Wipf and Stock, 2018), where I lay out the argument that the Fourth Gospel was originally written by a woman, most likely Mary Magdalen, that the majority of Luke's Gospel was written by a woman, quite possibly Mary of Bethany, who sat

sufficiently piqued that you will want to read the book, *"Three Certitudes About Jesus"*?

---

at the feet of Rabbi Yeshua; further, very much of Matthew's Gospel stems from a woman, either as from written or oral sources; even Mark's Gospel is heavily sourced from women. Take away all that we know of Yeshua that is sourced from women followers, there would such a weak picture of Yeshua that a religion about him would never have been born. Put positively: Rabbi Yeshua's Jewish women followers are the Founders of Christianity!

3. The Rabbi and the Adulteress

A similar situation occurred, Will, when Rabbi Yeshua was teaching at daybreak in the Temple precincts—Jeez, who voluntarily gets up before daybreak and goes to a Temple (or a church, for that matter) to listen to a teacher!? Yeshua must have had quite a reputation as a teacher! Not just that, Will. The Gospel states really broadly: "*All* the people came." Well, of course, it cannot mean all the people in the world, or even all the people in the city; it probably just means all sorts of different people—and everybody who was crazy enough to be up that early in the morning!

The Gospel then strangely reports that a group of Scribes and Pharisees used a woman just to set a "legal" trap for Yeshua [Jn. 8:2-11]—this abruptness tells us that this story does not really belong in this place—more about this below. Will, in talking about this "adulterous" woman used by the enemies of Rabbi Yeshua, it is difficult to imagine a more callous use of a human person. First of all, she was surprised by this group of Scribes and Pharisees in the intimate act of sexual intercourse.

The question absolutely suggests itself. Had a trap been set up ahead of time by the suspicious fiancé? The punishment they spoke of tells us that the woman was not yet married, but only "engaged," which nevertheless could still get her killed! Was the fiancé in cahoots with the Scribes and Pharisees??

The Rabbi and the Adulteress

For one wonders, Will: What was that bunch of Scribes and Pharisees doing sneaking around early in the morning on a deadly, salacious search? The woman and her chosen lover (not the one she presumably was being forced to marry by her family) were having their early morning secret tryst.

She was, doubtless…. Wait! Where was the "lover"? He was not brought to Rabbi Yeshua, or even mentioned in the Gospel. Did he somehow escape that whole gang of Scribes and Pharisees? The Gospel speaks of both the Scribes and Pharisees in the plural, so there had to be, at minimum, four, but probably more of them all together. Or, **was he just playing the role of a "seducer"** and was in on the plot?

It is an interesting possibility considering his **not being mentioned at all** in the Gospel story.

In any case, Will, *she* was dragged by the Scribes and Pharisees to the front of the large Temple crowd that Yeshua was teaching: "Making her stand in full view of everybody." They told Rabbi Yeshua that she had been caught in the very act of committing adultery (voluntary sexual intercourse between a married person and a person who is not his or her spouse] and that Moses had commanded that such women be stoned to death [Dt. 22:22]). "What have you to say?" It is hard not to imagine a smirk on their faces when they uttered this challenge.

Remember, the idea of the trap I wrote about earlier, was partly that if Yeshua said "Yes" to the stoning, he would be violating Roman law, which restricted capital punishment (sentenced to death) to the local Roman Procurator (an agent representing others in a court of law).

A second part of the trap was that, if he said "No, don't stone her," he would appear to violate Mosaic Law (the law of Moses). Furthermore, they may have used the adulteress woman as a tool to publicly show Yeshua's reputation for championing women by choosing not to condemn her.

Will, you can see that the Scribes and Pharisees were trying to set up a situation like a very "clever" lawyer. When in the courtroom, the lawyer says to the husband on the witness stand accused of beating his wife:

"Mr. Bully, yes or no, have you stopped beating your wife?" Of course, if he said "Yes... I stopped beating her," the lawyer would then say, "Aha! Then you *were* beating her!"

If, however, he said, "No... I did not stop beating her," the lawyer would then say, "Aha! Then you are still beating her!"

The Gospel here reports something quite strange, but really interesting. It says that Yeshua "then bent over and with his finger wrote in the sand." This is the only reference in the four Gospels to Rabbi Yeshua writing.

The Rabbi and the Adulteress

One ancient manuscript version of the Gospel at this point adds: "As if he had not heard them." However, the Gospel records then that the Scribes and Pharisees kept asking him.

They picked the wrong Rabbi to try their tricks on. He eluded their snares by refusing to become entangled in legalisms and abstractions. Rather, he dealt with both the accusers and the accused as ethical persons and spoke directly to the accusers about *their own* ethical conduct.

One wonders, Will, what Yeshua was writing? Why do you think the Gospel writer included this tasty tidbit? Hmm? Was Yeshua just playing for time to think? Was he writing some of the "sins" he knew the Pharisees were involved in? Was he writing some of their names??? Next, the Gospel states, "Rabbi Yeshua stood back up and said: 'If there is one of you who has not sinned, let him be the first to throw a stone at her.'"

Wow! Will, I am sure that there was a sort of stunned silence! Who was going to step forward and throw a rock at the woman, thereby claiming, "I have never done anything wrong!" Especially if Rabbi Yeshua had been writing in the sand some of the more prominent Scribes' and Pharisees' names…? We don't know, of course, but clearly the wind had gone out of their sails, for the Gospel says that the crowd "went away one by one, starting with the oldest." Yeshua's challenge was to all, not just the Scribes and Pharisees!

But why did "the oldest" leave first? Because they had more time to "sin?" A sticky question!

Now, Will, it is also very interesting to note that the Gospel tells us that Yeshua must have bent down again, waiting for someone to throw the first stone. What was going through the woman's mind at this point!? If you or I were in her place....? Yikes! Was he writing some more? We don't know, for the Gospel simply says that, after all had gone away, "Yeshua stood up again."

Presumably he left the answer to his question—about who was sinless enough to throw the first stone—to each person's conscience; perhaps he did not wish to embarrass them by looking each in the eye. A nice touch, eh, Will? Sort of killing them with kindness!

Then, of course, the woman was still standing there in the middle, where she had been dragged. The Gospel says that Yeshua then again stood up and looked at her and asked: "Where are they? Did no one condemn you?" She said, "No one, Rabbi." Yeshua's response was simple, and clear: "Neither will I condemn you. Go, and sin no more."

Did she, like the prostitute we just read about, throw herself at Rabbi Yeshua's feet—and weeping, blurt out, "Thank you! Thank you! Thank you!" The Gospel story tells us nothing of her response or departure. We are left to imagine ourselves into that ghastly near-miss situation, and try to conjure up what must have gone through her mind, what her raging emotions might have led her to do.

4. The Missing Story!

Think about it! The story must have spread like wildfire. This event broke all the rules! That very young girl was supposed to be dead! As an engaged girl she would have been in her early teens, younger than you, Will! Somehow this new, spell-binding Rabbi Yeshua quietly shamed all the men into slinking away, and then let her go scot-free! Remember, this happened right there in the Temple precincts (neighborhood) where Rabbi Yeshua was teaching a crowd of people.

However, the story also burnt like wildfire in another way—for it is **not found at all** in the earliest manuscripts we possess. It apparently "burnt the hands of the copyists so fiercely" that they could not bring themselves to copy it from the original manuscript. And further, when it does appear in later Gospel manuscripts, it ends up not where it was first in the Gospel of Luke, but in the fourth Gospel, traditionally attributed to someone named John. As I intimated earlier, I and a small but growing group of scholars are convinced it was written not by some "John," but by a woman, and most likely Mary Magdalene[5], Yeshua's very close companion. However, it is a universally held scholarly position that it was definitely not written by the fourth Gospel writer—but was for some reason ripped out of Luke's

---

[5] See footnote 4.

The Missing Story!

Gospel at Chapter 5, verse 38 where it was originally written and ended up at John in Chapter 8, verses 2-11!

Why, Will, do you suppose this dramatic story almost got totally lost? Well, think about it.... Here was Rabbi Yeshua not only contradicting the Torah, but he was, in effect, condoning adultery!

Now, you might be thinking, 'Well, practically all religions have strong limiting rules about sex.' Well, yes, religions in general can often have rigid boundaries about sex.

However, ask yourself, how come there was no difficulty in keeping the story about the prostitute? More, why was the adulteress not also condemned to be stoned to death? She was having sex with many men, none of whom were her husband!

Ah, yes. But the greatest evil was not in having extra-marital sex as that apparently was just an "ordinary" (but necessary?) evil. Adultery was one man **stealing** another man's property—his wife! Apparently, the worse evil was stealing!

Let me end our look at this story, Will, by recalling once again what Rabbi Yeshua said to the woman after everyone else left. He did not read her the riot act or anything like it. Of course, Will, she hardly needed that since she had already been scared half to death! Rabbi Yeshua *really* did go beyond the Law of Moses by treating her with forgiveness, saying that he would not condemn her, but that she should learn the lesson and commit no further wrongs.

If you think about everything you know about Yeshua, Will, you find that he never ever talks about some evil being punished by death. Never! Forgiveness? "How often?" he was asked by his followers. "Seven times?" they wanted to know. Nope, seventy times seven! he said.

So, yes, the disapproving copyist was right in thinking that this story, as he read it, had Rabbi Yeshua changing the old rules, eliminating the death penalty, and therefore suppressed this story. Presumably he was thinking something like: "My holy Rabbi Yeshua could *never* have substituted mushy-thinking mercy and forgiveness for righteous justice, even if it included a just death penalty!"

Oops! Sorry, my friend the copyist, that is precisely what Rabbi Yeshua did—embarrassing as that was to you and still is to many Christians alive today.

5. Jesus Really Was a Feminist—So…?

Will, just from the couple of stories I laid out only to some degree, you should get the picture that Rabbi Yeshua was really swimming against the current. His positive, feminist attitude and even more, his bold, risky actions levelled the playing field for women in his society. We looked ever so briefly at just two episodes in which Yeshua went way out on a limb supporting culturally-despised women. He showed his commitment and courage knowing he would offend powerful men. These men oppressed women and in one instance even threatened their death.

In his widespread healing and teaching (even at sunrise at the Temple!) he had obviously gained a lot of so-called "social capital," meaning widespread goodwill. Will, we found increasingly large numbers of people —especially women, but also men coming to hear him at sunrise at the Temple. Further, he was more than willing to spend his social capital by defending the most defenseless of women. He appears to have no concern about the potential cost to himself. There is much more to spell out further if you are interested!

6. Looking Forward

Will, I would like to hear back from you, before I go any further down this path of Rabbi Yeshua as a *feminist*—two thousand years before his time! In any case, let me know what you think about what I wrote or important points you think I missed or somehow messed up. There is a lot more that can be said about Rabbi Yeshua and his extraordinary feminist thought and action—which got him in big trouble.

Auf Wiedersehen! [German for until we meet again.]

Opa

- **Letters to Will Series** -

Letter 6:
JESUS WAS A RABBI—OMG!

A Grandfather's Guide to Life

Leonard Swidler, PhD (Grandfather)

Letters to Will Series: Book 6

Letter 6: Jesus Was a Rabbi—OMG!

Leonard Swidler (grandfather)

This book is available as an individual volume. Visit
https://ipubcloud.com/product/letter-6-jesus-was-a-rabbi-omg/

Contents

1. Who Should Be Interested in
Whether Jesus Was a Jew? 1

2. God is "Echad," One! 3

3. Creation is "*Tov*," Humans are "*Mod Tov*" 5

4. Rabbi Yeshua WAS Most Interested in Society's
Marginalized Outcasts 7

5. Malkut Shomaim – the "Rule of Heaven" 9

6. Malkut Shomaim – A Female God? 11

7. A Transformed Person and Society 13

8. For Greeks, the Big Question was, What to Think? For
Jews: What to Do? 15

9. Yeshua's Teaching of the Goal—Malkut Shomaim 17

10. The Picture Language Jews—and Rabbi Yeshua—Used:
Fatally Misunderstood! 19

11. Summary 22

Dear Will,

In my last letter to you, I noted to you that Jesus, the "Foundation" of Christianity, wasn't even a Christian, but was a Jew! In a kind of throw-away remark, you wrote back, "that's kinda weird." Then you added a quizzical question that has been itching in my brain since then: "Does it make any difference that Jesus was not Christian, but Jewish?"

1. Who Should Be Interested in Whether Jesus Was a Jew?

Actually, Will, the more I thought about it, the more I became convinced that it wasn't really just a throw-away remark or flip question. It shines a light on a very deep and troubling--two-thousand-year-old problem.

Also, Will, yours is not a question that only Christians should follow up on! No, it is clear to me that most of the rest of the world should also probe the question. After all, Christians in 2010 numbered 2.2 billion out of a world total of 6.9 billion—almost a third of the global population! In that number of people who should be interested, Will, we should obviously include the global Jewish population of 15 million—precisely because Jesus was Jewish. In fact, he was the most influential Jew in all of history! (Runners-up would include Karl Marx, Sigmund Freud, and Albert Einstein.) Further, we should also include the 1.6 billion Muslims in the world, for the Qur'an reverently refers to

Who Should Be Interested in Whether Jesus Was a Jew?

Jesus (*Isa*) as the *al-Masih* (Messiah), and explicitly mentions with great respect his mother Mary (*Maryam*) more often than any other woman (in fact, the Qur'an even has a whole chapter named *Maryam*, after her!)

All these together make up almost 4 billion (roughly 70%) out of the total number of people living in 2010! So, Will, whether one is 1) a Christian (or *former* Christian—and perhaps especially them!), 2) a Jew, 3) a Muslim—4) an agnostic, or 5) even a "raving atheist," for most often they both are thus, consciously or not, rejecting the Christianity they grew up in, or around them—they should all care about Jesus. What Jesus thought of himself—and what his first followers thought of him—should be fundamental questions for them!

I hear you, Will; you are thinking: why should they care? Well, Will, in short--the modern world, for good and ill--has been massively formed and shaped by Western Civilization, which has as one of its core elements Christianity—built on Jesus of Nazareth—who wasn't even a Christian!

Will, in an earlier letter where we learned that "Jesus was a Feminist," I wrote that in the rest of that letter I was going to use the Hebrew form of Jesus' name, *Yeshua*, as a conscious help for us moderns to remember that he was not a Greek or a Roman (*Jesus* is the Latin form of the Greek *Iesous*, which in turn is a translation of the Hebrew *Yeshua*—meaning "God, *Yahweh*, saves"). He was a Jew!

2. God is "Echad," One!

So, Will, what's one of the first things we think of when we think about Yeshua being a Jew and not a Greek or Roman? Well, Greeks and Romans, and everybody else, were polytheists; only the Jews claimed that there is just *one* source of everything that exists, including all humans. That means that despite all the differences among humans, as the very beginning of the Bible claims, all humans are to be treated with the *same* rules, for they all were created by the *same*, the *one* God. God is, as said in the most important Jewish prayer recited every day by devout Jews, *Echad*, One!

Shema Yisrael Yahweh Eloheinu Yahweh Echad!

Remember O Israel; Yahweh—our God Yahweh—is One!

3. Creation is *"Tov,"* Humans are *"Mod Tov"*

And here's the clincher, Will; the very first book of the Bible states that at the end of each day of creation "God saw that what he had done was good" (*Tov* in Hebrew). Further, at the end of the sixth day, when God created humanity, the Bible states that "God saw that what he had done was "very good." (*Mod Tov*).

Now, Will, I can just hear you saying that millions of modern people don't think that the world was created in six days! True enough, Will. In fact, hundreds of millions of Christians don't either! The important point, Will, is that the vast majority of Western Europeans, most of whom were Christian, did until less than a couple of hundred years ago (1859, Charles Darwin's *Origin of Species*), and they shaped their (our!) civilization accordingly. That meant, Will, that the basic thrust of developing Christian/Western Civilization had at its foundation the claim that *all* humans, precisely because they came from *one* (*Echad*) source, should be treated "very well," *Mod Tov*.

There are other ways, of course, to understand that all humans are the equivalent of *Mod Tov* than Biblical religion. But, Will, the important point here is that this idea that *all* humans are *Mod Tov* has been spread around the whole world in substantial ways by the followers of this Biblical religion; by Christians and their cultural descendants.

Creation is "Tov," Humans are "Mod Tov"

Again Will, I hear you thinking that an awful lot of so-called followers of the Bible, Christians, didn't follow that teaching at all! That is clearly still is true in 2019—one need only think of how the current president of our country horribly mistreats everyone different from him (clearly, he does not think that any non-white Christians are even *Tov*, let alone, *Mod Tov*!—and is still followed by millions of so-called "evangelical," (from the Greek of the New Testament, *Evangelion*, "Gospel"?!) Christians. Those "Others" clearly are not seen by these Christians as *Mod Tov*!

Nevertheless, Will, hundreds of millions of other Christians do follow, for example, the banner of Pope Francis (and not just Catholics) in constantly urging care and concern for multiple others, especially the poor and oppressed, for they indeed are *Mod Tov*.

Hence, both the Christians and the rest of the world need to attend to the fact that the fundamental teaching—and example—of Rabbi Yeshua was essentially *Jewish* when he reached out to and treated especially the sick, poor, and marginalized (women, *Jesus Was a Feminist!*) as *Mod Tov*, indeed.

4. Rabbi Yeshua WAS Most Interested in Society's Marginalized Outcasts

One of the greatest contributions Western Civilization, the "offspring" of Christendom, has made to the whole world is the notion, and growing reality, of human rights, essentially meaning that all humans are to be treated as *Mod Tov*! Yes, Will, it took a long, long time for Westerners (including Christians!) to realize that all humans came from one Source, and that they were created *Mod Tov*. There is embedded the glorious modern message that *every* person has built-in fundamental human rights (hence, also responsibilities).

Then, Will, many Christian thinkers, theologians, and activists looked to the example of Rabbi Yeshua spending his adult life teaching, healing the sick, and "hanging out with" outcasts: The poor, lepers, despised, women, children—those not considered by society and its leaders as being *Mod Tov*. Will, those Christians took their inspiration from that Jewish Rabbi Yeshua and launched a multiple-pronged movement in many cultures and languages, in general, called "Liberation Theology." These Christian followers of Rabbi Yeshua did not spend their energy creating an abstract philosophy. No, they provided a rationale and inspiration that followed Rabbi Yeshua in actions that aimed at changing, not just individuals, but whole structures of society: One that would treat everyone as *Mod Tov*.

5. Malkut Shomaim – the "Rule of Heaven"

Will, that Jewish rabbi was a pretty amazing guy! He put together and launched, not so much a theory, but an *action* plan that was at the same time deep, profoundly thought-through, as well as tested and worked-out in action. When you re-read the Gospels—which focus mainly on Rabbi *Yeshua*, not on *Christ* (that's St. Paul's special focus), on his teaching and his actions, that is, his putting his teaching into everyday *action*—you will notice a key term that he very frequently used: The *Reign of God*. You doubtless are asking yourself, "What in the world does that mean, especially in today's world?" Well, it again goes back to that pair of terms that describe both *everything* in the world as "good" (*Tov*), and all humans, as "very good" (*Mod Tov*).

Actually, Will, in the Hebrew language that Yeshua spoke, the term used was the "Rule of *Heaven*," *Malkut Shomaim*. Hmm, what do you think, Will? Do you agree that that's a little closer to our twenty-first century kind of language? Today we sometimes speak of "the heavens," meaning the cosmos, the universe (shades of our recent discovery of the Big Bang!). I think it suggests that there is a Heavenly order to the universe, cosmos, and that is what we humans should follow.

You know, Will, it's like the basic rules of ethics, which, as we saw in an earlier letter, if too many people in a community don't follow them, that society will destroy itself. For example, if everybody thought that it was OK to kill anybody they didn't like for one reason or another, pretty soon everybody would be dead except the "strongest" man, who would also eventually die. Then, what happens next, Will? Poof! That society is *Gone*!

Obviously, only those societies exist today which basically followed fundamental "do and don't" rules, like "Don't kill innocent persons"—the rest killed themselves off! Well, Will, you ask then: what was meant by Rabbi Yeshua's "*Rule* of Heaven," *Malkut Shomaim*?

6. Malkut Shomaim – A Female God?

Will, before I talk about how Yeshua understood this key term for him, *Malkut Shomaim*, because I know that you are something of a history buff, let me describe in passing a very interesting short video clip that I stumbled across on YouTube. It is about the very ancient use of the title *Malkut Shomaim* as it appeared in the fifth-century BCE Jewish colony in northern Egypt, Elephantine, and at the same time in Judea.

The interesting link is:

https://youtu.be/48TeNWCfHuA

Malkut Shomaim in Elephantine Judaism (a fortress state in northern Egypt settled by Jews) and in Judea of fifth-century BCE referred to a Jewish female God! Hence, at that time and place it meant not the "*Rule* of Heaven," but the "*Queen* of Heaven," later Christianized *Regina Coeli* in Latin, which you may well have sung in church!

Now Will, calm down! Yes, a lot of Jews in those ancient days did worship a female God! Just go get your Bible and turn to Jeremiah 44:15-19, where you see that the prophet roundly condemned those Jews who adored the female *Malkut Shomaim*. But the women stoutly stood their ground, saying to the Prophet that when they worshipped the *Queen of Heaven*, everything was just wonderful, thank you very much!

Malkut Shomaim – A Female God?

Of course, Will, things did not continue to go so well for them, and eventually Judaism fell into one political or military disaster after another. So, after the Jews were dragged into exile in Babylon in the fifth-century BCE, 70 years later they were allowed to return to Judea and put together the *Torah*, the Pentateuch, that is, the first five books of the Bible. And Will, from that time onward the whole Jewish population was committed to true monotheism. And so, also from then on *Malkut Shomaim* was understood as the *Rule of Heaven*.

So now Will, let me go back to the question you put to me: "What was meant by Rabbi Yeshua's *Rule* of Heaven, *Malkut Shomaim*"?

Responding to that question somewhat completely would take a whole book or more. You will remember, Will, that we already touched on it in a way in our earlier letters. However, since we started today talking specifically about Yeshua being a Jew (and a rabbi to boot!), I pointed out that throughout his teaching we find him constantly coming back to this very Jewish idea and term of the "Rule of Heaven," *Malkut Shomaim*.

7. A Transformed Person and Society

It was apparently a much-discussed issue in Yeshua's time for he is recorded having said about the *Malkut Shomaim*: "Some say 'it is here, some say that it is there!'" But no, Yeshua said that the "Rule of Heaven" is *"entos hymon."* That's the original Greek of the Gospel. The second term, *hymon*, means "you." What is really interesting, Will, is that the term, *entos*, means *both* "within" *and* "among." In other words, Rabbi Yeshua was teaching that the "Rule of Heaven" is both *within* you and *among* you. You can see, Will, that Yeshua was making the dual point that you 1) needed to make the "Heavenly Rule" absolutely real *within* you. However, you could not follow the "Rule of Heaven" *only* individually, *entos*, *"within"* yourself, but it also needed to be 2) *entos*, *"among,"* communally, yourselves!

So, you see, Will, Yeshua was pushing two very Jewish things: 1) Making human persons better one by one, *and* 2) working at changing the societal culture—increasingly fostering structures of society that will foster the "Rule of Heaven" so that *individual* persons will be taught and encouraged by the *community* to live within the *Malkut Shomaim*!

Think, Will, the first prayer that a Christian is taught is the so-called Lord's Prayer. It starts out: "Our Father who art in heaven (*Shomaim*), thy Kingdom (Rule, *Malkut*) come, thy will be done on Earth…." Of course, Will, the "Lord," after whom this quintessential Jewish prayer is named is none other than The Jew Rabbi Yeshua!

8. For Greeks, the Big Question was, What to Think? For Jews: What to Do?

Will, that emphasis by Rabbi Yeshua (I hope that by now you are beginning to *feel* comfortable with the fact that Yeshua was not a Christian but was a Jew!) leads us to notice that he was very, very different from the great Greek philosophers with whom we in the West are so familiar, like Socrates, Plato, and Aristotle. For them—and the Greek culture in general—the *big* question was: What should I *think*? One of the first things the Christians (by that time they were by far mostly Greek speakers/thinkers) did when they gained freedom in the Roman Empire was to create, at the first Ecumenical (Universal) Council at Nicaea in 325 CE, a very detailed *Credo* (Latin, "I believe.") That is, Will, they hammered out what Christians should *think*.

Further, Will, let me ask you another question. I'm sure you know the answer: what were the four faculties of the great medieval Christian universities founded upon in the High Middle Ages—like at Paris, Oxford, Cambridge, Bologna, and one of my Alma Mater's, Tubingen? The answer, of course, is Philosophy, Theology, Law, and Medicine. Notice, the first three were all about how we humans should *think*! And, if you didn't think the right way, you could be burned at the stake!

Will, let's have a little test: What is the Jewish *Credo*? I know that you know from visiting a number of synagogue services with Jewish friends. Before I remind you of the

For Greeks, the Big Question was...

answer--we already spoke of it above--let me also recall that for centuries, traditional Jews have out a sense of respect avoided speaking out loud the *personal* name of God—*Yahweh* (which means: *I will be who I will be*)—but substitute for it the Hebrew word *Adonai*, Lord.

The answer, Will, as you've often heard recited, is *Shema Yisrael Adonai Eloheinu Adonai Echad!* "Remember O Israel, the Lord [*Yahweh*] our God, the Lord [*Yahweh*] is one." That's it! That's all you have to believe philosophically. However, there are hundreds of rules of *action* that you have to *do*. So, for the Greeks, the *big* (not the only) question was: "What must I *think*? But for the Jews, the *big* (not the only) question was: What must *I do*?

Will, I know that you have read at least part of the Gospels and have heard chunks of them read at the Christian services where you sang in your fantastic choirs. Think of what you know of the Gospels—not the letters of St. Paul and other parts of the New Testament. What are they about? The answer, of course, is that the four Gospels are all focused on Yeshua and his *teaching* and *actions*, helping....who? We saw, Will, that it was the marginalized; the outcasts of society. And what did he do with them? As seen above, we noted that he cured the sick, fed the hungry, and most of all, taught them that they were personally worthwhile (*Mod Tov*) and that they, whatever their place in life and society, should attempt to live the *Malkut Shomaim*, the "Rule of Heaven."

9. Yeshua's Teaching of the Goal—Malkut Shomaim

Will, every semester I teach a class on world religions. When I get to Christianity, I, of course, start with its founder, Rabbi Yeshua (I have to work a bit to get them used to making the connection between the terms Jesus and Yeshua!). I ask them, or at least the Christians in the class, "What did Yeshua say was the key to the reward for a good life?" They then usually come up with answers like, "Believe in Jesus as your Savior," "Avoid mortal sins," "Go to church on Sundays," etc., etc. Then I ask them, "Where is it recorded that Yeshua connected one or another of those things with, as he put it sometimes: Receive the reward, enter into heaven?" Of course, he didn't. Yeshua, as a *Mod Tov* Jew, said what, Will? Definitely "Not those who *say* 'Lord, Lord,' but those who *do* the will of my Father will enter into the reward that he has been prepared for you." And what is the "Will of my Father"? I quote Yeshua directly: "Feed the hungry, give drink to the thirsty, clothe the naked, visit the sick, visit those in prison...."

Again, Will, it is very clear that Rabbi Yeshua was not a Greek, a Roman, a Persian, but an essential *Jew*, focusing not on what to believe or *think*, but on what to *do*, as the *big* question! Will, Yeshua, as a *Mod Tov* Jew, made it clear that "Not those who *say*, 'Lord, Lord,' but who *do* the will of my Father will live in the *Malkut Shomaim!*"

Yeshua's Teaching of the Goal—Malkut Shomaim

Again, Will, remember, one should not assume that Yeshua was saying, "Hang in there, things may be miserable for you now, but after you die, it will be just wonderful!" As we saw, he said that the *Malkut Shomaim* is "not *here* or *there*" (this life or afterlife), but is *entos hymon*, both within and among you—and you can make it starting *now* and *continuing*....

10. The Picture Language Jews and Rabbi Yeshua Used: Fatally Misunderstood!

Will, you have read hundreds, and by now, probably thousands of books of all kinds, from serious ones to fantasy novels. Hence, by now you automatically recognize when some writing is to be taken at face value and others in some kind of expanded, transformed sense. Some writing is meant as factual, and some as metaphorical, or symbolic. Well, Will, I want to suggest that not everybody all the time recognized that difference that you do. Further, I want to point out that two thousand years ago when Yeshua lived, the vast majority of Jews could not read. Hence, if you wanted to influence them, you did not sit down and write books or newspaper articles (there were none then!). No, Will, you had to go out and tell stories that would capture the attention of the masses of unlettered persons (the Gospels tell of when Rabbi Yeshua taught crowds of several thousands!). The way I like to describe that way of speaking is to say that it tends to use *Picture Language*.

Will, that is precisely the sort of language Yeshua, as a good rabbi, used with the crowds of people who went to hear him teach. This was totally different from the way famous Greek philosophers spoke with their followers. They wrote many books (as far as we know, Rabbi Yeshua wrote zero!). They did not teach large crowds in great open spaces like Yeshua; rather, for example, the famous philosopher Plato created his *Akademia*; his equally famous student Aristotle was the head of the *Lykeion*. Both were

The Picture Language Jews and Rabbi Yeshua Used

places of scholarly thinking, writing, teaching of small groups of intellectuals—and whose names, *Academy* and *Lyceum*, we still use for institutions of higher learning.

Dear Will, as you know from your own reading, these and other Greek institutions were places of careful scientific and abstract philosophic thought—the very opposite of the way most of the Bible, as well as Jewish thought and writing in general, was carried out. For example, what do you suppose the Jew John the Baptist, a cousin of Yeshua, meant when, as recorded in the Fourth Gospel, one day he was talking with two of his disciples (i.e., students) and saw Yeshua walking by and said to them: "Look, the lamb of God." Do you suppose he meant that Yeshua was a white wooly four-legged animal? Of course not. You would say, the "lamb of God" must have had symbolic meaning to them—which the disciples understood, for they then immediately went and followed Rabbi Yeshua.

Or again, Will, what do you suppose Yeshua meant when he said to a group of Jews: "If your eye leads you astray, poke it out!"? Do you think that he meant that if any of his followers looked at something they shouldn't, they should actually poke their eye out!? Well, if so, there would be a lot more Christians with eyepatches in the world! Of course, he meant the poking metaphorically. Yeshua, like a good Jew, was speaking the way he knew the Jewish crowds were thinking—in *Picture Language*!

Will, you are probably thinking about now, "OK, Yeshua, and Jews in general, spoke in *Picture Language*—so?" The answer to "So?" is at first the obvious answer: If we want to understand what Rabbi Yeshua (and the Jewish Bible) meant in his teachings, we need to recognize that his teaching is couched in that kind of *Picture Language*, and not in either the concrete or abstract language the Greeks tended to use with such great depth.

Now, Will, I can hear you saying to yourself: Got it! Well, an awful lot of people—I really mean mainly Christians—didn't, and still don't, get it! For example, in one of the Gospels, it is recorded that some listener was really so impressed by Yeshua's teaching and actions that he said to him, "You are the son of God!" Wow! That sounds like this Jew meant that Yeshua was really a son of God—like a Greek would think that Apollo was "really" (or, to use a Greek-rooted technical term, ontologically) a son of the god Zeus. But, Will, we need to ask, is that what a Jew would mean by saying that "Yeshua was a son of God"? Not at all! When we read the Bible and other Jewish writings of the time, we find that to be a "son of God" meant that you are doing what God wants you to do—or, as was said in old-fashioned English, "you are a *godly* person."

This reading of Jewish *Picture Language* or *Ontological Language* as if it were *real*, is to badly *mis*read it—Yeshua did not go around saying "baaaa!" He did not mean to say what a Greek would *mis*understand--that he was a god like Apollo. Will, I can "hear" you going very silent, thinking about what a huge difference this makes in how to understand the Bible and all the teaching of Yeshua in a correct—Jewish!—way, if we want to "get it," and not to "get it wrong!"

11. Summary

So, Will, we have really covered a lot of ground in this letter, which started with the question: What difference does it make that Yeshua was a rabbi? I pointed out that there were fundamental reasons why practically *everybody* should pay attention to the fact that Yeshua was a Jew. Then, Will, we saw that in the time of Yeshua the Jewish message of *one* God, *Echad*, who created everything, including *all* humans provided a basis for the development of the idea of *human rights* for all! In addition to the key term *Echad*, we looked at the important story at the very beginning of the Bible and saw that it said that everything that exists was created by God as "good," *Tov*, and that humans are *"very* good," *Mod Tov*. This provided another breakthrough notion eventually leading to the claim that *all* reality is *good*, and that all humans are not only good, *Tov*, but even very good, *Mod Tov!*

Then, Will, we began to focus on Rabbi Yeshua and saw that, because he took extremely seriously the Jewish notion that *all* humans are *Mod Tov*, he spent much of his teaching life hanging out with the outcasts of society precisely because he saw them as *Mod Tov!* Then, Will, we focused on another key term and insight of Yeshua, the "Rule of Heaven," *Malkut Shomaim*. We saw that it was no longer thought of as the *Queen of Heaven* (or, did it still secretly retain something of that feminine quality?), nor as some after-death heaven, but that it started here and now, and was both *in* you, and *among* you—*entos hymon*. This dual understanding of the *Rule of Heaven* taught that each person is *Mod Tov, very good*, and should be treated as such, both individually and through transformed societal structures which treated everyone as *Mod Tov*.

Related to that, Will, is the fact that for the Greeks the *big* question is "What must I *think*?" whereas the *big* question for Jews is "What must I *do*?" The answer for Jews was to follow the "Rule of Heaven," *Malkut Shomaim*. How? Each person followed this both *within* her/himself and *among*, societal structures, each other, thereby transforming each person and society as a whole.

Last, but by no means least, Will, we briefly investigated the critical issue of language. We saw that the Jewish language was fundamentally *Picture Language*, and was very different from the Greek language which tended to be abstract. This significant difference in the use of language, and how to properly understand it, has frequently led to a *mis*understanding of what the Bible, and Rabbi Yeshua, taught and embodied.

So yes, Will, the fact that Jesus was a Jew, was Rabbi Yeshua, makes a hell—whoops, I mean, (Rule of) *Heaven* of a lot of difference!

Dein, Opa

Don't Miss Out on Other Books in This Series.

Visit https://ipubcloud.com/ to learn about other world-renowned authors.

Click on the images of links to the website.

Letters to Will Series

Letter 3: What Is Global Ethic?
A Grandfather's Guide to Life

Leonard Swidler, PhD (Grandfather)

Letters to Will Series

Letter 4: What is Buddhism?
A Grandfather's Guide to Life

Leonard Swidler, PhD (Grandfather)

www.ingramcontent.com/pod-product-compliance
Lightning Source LLC
Chambersburg PA
CBHW070052070426
42449CB00012BA/3241